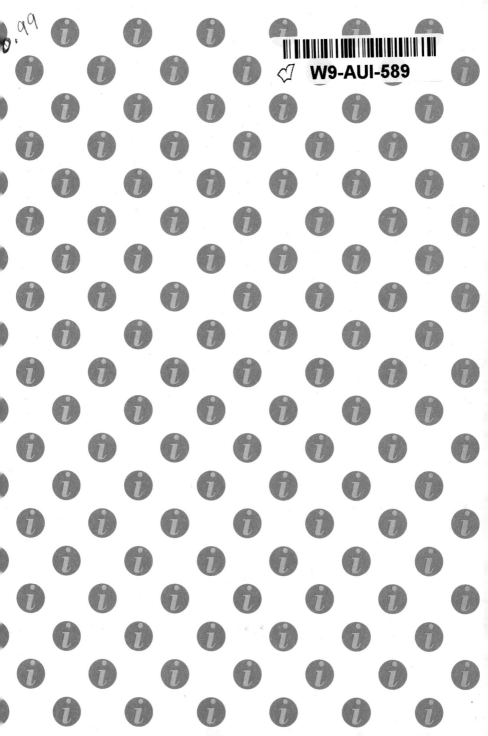

0.99

W9-AUI-589

IDENTIFYING

FROGS

& TOADS

The new compact study guide and identifier

IDENTIFYING

i

FROGS
& TOADS

The new compact study guide and identifier

Ken Preston-Mafham

CHARTWELL
BOOKS, INC.

A QUINTET BOOK

Published by Chartwell Books
A Division of Book Sales, Inc.
114 Northfield Avenue
Edison, New Jersey 08837

This edition produced for sale
in the U.S.A., its territories
and dependencies only.

ISBN 0-78581-110-9

This book was designed and published by
Quintet Publishing Limited
6 Blundell Street
London N7 9BH

Creative Director: Richard Dewing
Designer: Rod Teasdale
Project Editor: Amanda Dixon
Editor: Maggie O'Hanlon
Illustration: Paul Richardson and Ann Savage

Typeset in Great Britain by
Central Southern Typesetters, Eastbourne
Manufactured in Hong Kong by Regent Publishing Services Ltd
Printed in Singapore by Star Standard Industries Pte Ltd

All photography reproduced by permission of Chris Mattison,
Ken Preston-Mafham, Dr. Rod Preston-Mafham, and
Jean Preston-Mafham for Premaphotos Wildlife.

CONTENTS

INTRODUCTION

It was not so long ago that frogs and toads seemed to be almost universally condemned as loathsome, slimy creatures. Fortunately, the growth in interest in wildlife and its conservation has led to an increasing perception that all wild animals are of interest and value, and that their welfare should be the concern of every thinking person. Fortunately this positive change in attitude also encompasses frogs and toads, which are now welcomed in a garden pond, rather than discouraged. The keeping of frogs and toads as pets, particularly some of the brilliantly colored exotic species, has also snowballed in recent years, introducing an ever-widening band of people to the beauty and interest of these creatures.

What Is a Frog and What Is a Toad?

There is no clearcut answer to this. The difference in terminology arose long ago when the name "frog" was applied to the common frog of Europe (*Rana temporaria*), while the name "toad" was reserved for another common European species, the common toad (*Bufo bufo*). Since then the names frog and toad have been applied almost indiscriminately, and although all members of the family Bufonidae are called toads, when we come to a family such as the Microhylidae, some members are called frogs and others toads.

Whether frog or toad, all these animals belong to the class of animals called Amphibia, which also includes newts and salamanders. Within the Amphibia, the frogs

Above The tadpoles can be clearly seen developing inside these eggs of the red-eyed tree frog (*Agalychnis callidryas*) in Costa Rica.

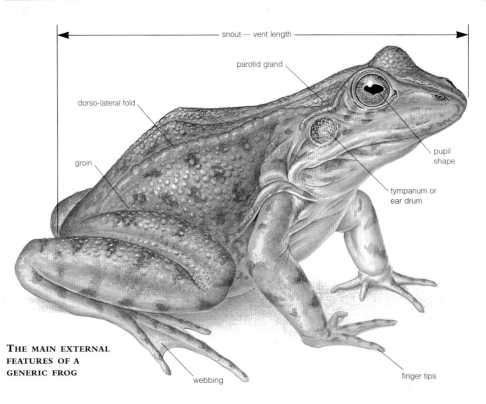

snout — vent length

parotid gland

dorso-lateral fold

pupil
shape

groin

tympanum or
ear drum

**THE MAIN EXTERNAL
FEATURES OF A
GENERIC FROG**

webbing

finger tips

and toads are included in the order Anura,
and it is often convenient to lump frogs
and toads together, and simply talk about
anurans. The Anura is divided into some 20
families (the number varies according to
which specialist you follow), and within
the families there is a further division into
genus and species. Thus, the genus of the
American bullfrog is *Rana,* and the species
is *catesbeiana*. Following convention, these
last two names are always italicized when
mixed with plain text. Of the 20 families,
examples from 14 are included in this
book, leaving out only six very small and
obscure families, some of which only
include two or three rare species.

Biology of Frogs and Toads

Anuran skin is permeable to water, which
constantly escapes via evaporation, so most
anurans live in damp places where evaporation is reduced and free water is usually
available for moistening the skin. However,
some frogs are amazingly resistant to
drying-out, particularly some African
species, which spend all day under a
roasting sun.

Most anurans "sing," although this occurs
almost exclusively in the males. Many
species have an expandable throat sac which
acts as an amplifier. Eggs are generally laid
and fertilized while the male lies on the
female's back and clasps her around the

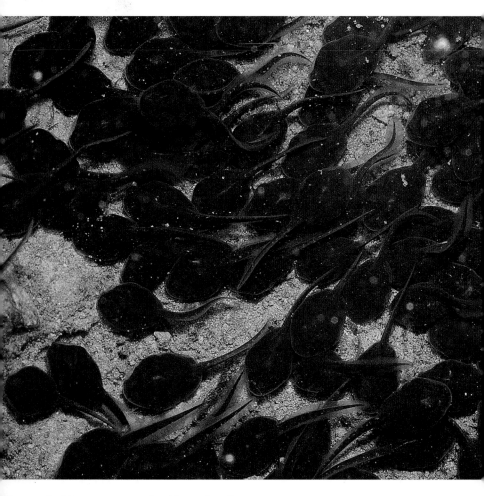

waist. The eggs are mostly rather soft and jellylike and easily dry-out, so are normally deposited in a moist place. This can be almost anywhere, including the back of the adult frog, as some of the descriptions will explain. The tadpoles have tails and gradually develop into tiny froglets. In some species these also have long tails for a while before they are finally absorbed.

Above Many tadpoles live in water, such as these of the giant toad (*Bufo marinus*) in Trinidad.

Above right This glass frog (*Centrolenella* sp.) has emerged from the aquatic tadpole stage with its long tail still intact.

What Do Frogs and Toads Eat?

All frogs and toads are predators, and they eat their victims alive. They grab, gulp, and crush their prey, swallowing it whole. A few frogs snap up only one kind of food, such as termites. Others eat almost any living creature that they can stuff into their wide, gaping mouths. Small animals without backbones, such as insects, spiders, and worms, are the mainstay of the diet. The bigger the frog, the bigger the prey it can tackle. Very large frogs, such as bullfrogs and marine toads, can eat mice, small rats, baby birds, lizards, and snakes. In the water, big frogs devour fish, pondworms, watersnails, and even small crabs.

Where Are Frogs and Toads Found?

There are about 4,000 species of frogs and toads currently recognized worldwide, with new species being described every year. As with so many different kinds of creatures, South America is the richest single area, with over 1,600 species. Of these, more than 100 species have been found in one area of northeastern Peru alone, some four times the total for the whole of Europe.

Unlike truly ubiquitous creatures, such as insects, frogs and toads cannot just be found anywhere. They tend to be patchily distributed and more abundant in some areas than others. Rainforests head the list,

Above The juveniles of some frogs can be confusingly different from the adult. This is a juvenile geographical tree frog (*Hyla geographica*). Compare it with the adult illustrated on p. 40

followed by swamps, damp grasslands, and woodlands. However, even deserts can boast quite a rich fauna of drought-adapted species, and many other kinds are found on high mountains. Few species are active in daytime, but nevertheless they can often be found during the day, either resting on leaves or bark, or concealed under stones, logs, planks, and bits of old iron. Many tree frogs in particular are easily found in daytime, although their colors may not be as rich as they become after dark.

How to Use The Identifier

The species described in this book are
arranged in family groups: fire-bellied
toads, painted frogs, and midwife toads;
aquatic frogs; spadefoots, horned toads,
etcetera; shovelfoot frogs, turtle frogs,
etcetera; wide-mouthed frogs, false-eyed
frogs, etcetera; true toads; slippery frogs;
tree frogs; glass frogs; poison-arrow frogs;
true frogs; sedge and reed frogs; old world
tree frogs; narrow-mouthed frogs.

Key to Symbols

The symbols given below accompany each entry and are intended to give vital information, at a
glance, about the behavior, habitat, and conservation status of the frog or toad.

When is the frog or toad active?

At night

By day

Note that this is when the frog is likely to be
active, that is calling, mating, laying eggs,
etcetera. Many anurans, especially tree frogs, are
easily found at rest during the day.

Where is the frog or toad likely to be found?

In or near, bogs, swamps, ponds,
lakes, rivers, etcetera

Rainforest

Mountains

Woodlands

Prairies,
savannahs,
scrublands,
etcetera

Around houses, in vacant lots, along
roadsides etcetera

Deserts

Where is the frog or toad most likely to be sitting?

Under a stone, log, plank, or discarded
rubbish, or in a burrow (mostly at night
in the dry season)

On the
ground

On a
treetrunk

On a leaf

In water

What is the frog's or toad's conservation status?

Common

Local, perhaps common where found,
but not widespread

Rare, very localized

FIRE-BELLIED TOADS, PAINTED FROGS, AND MIDWIFE TOADS

Family Discoglossidae

This is a very small and rather primitive family
containing only 11 species. These are of such varied
appearance that outwardly they would seem to have little
in common. However, a look inside the mouth would
reveal that they all possess a disk-shaped tongue that
cannot be extended beyond the lips. Distribution
is restricted to Europe and Asia.

MIDWIFE TOAD
ALYTES OBSTETRICANS

DESCRIPTION This small, rather rotund toad normally measures less than 1⁹⁄₁₆ in/ 48 mm in length. The eyes protrude quite prominently, and the pupil is vertical. The color is variable, mostly gray, olive, or brown, usually with a sprinkling of small dark markings, often green. Although superficially similar to some spadefoots (*Pelobates*), the lack of a spade on the hind foot is diagnostic. The parsley frog (*Pelodytes punctatus*) is similar, but much slimmer and with longer legs. In parts of Spain and Portugal lives the very similar Iberian midwife toad (*A. cisternasii*). This has three tubercles on the palm of the hand, instead of two, as in the midwife toad. Male midwife toads carry the eggs about, wrapped around their legs.

DISTRIBUTION Western Europe, eastward as far as Germany. Some small colonies survive in Britain after introductions by man.

YELLOW-BELLIED TOAD
BOMBINA VARIEGATA

DESCRIPTION This small gray, brown, olive, or yellowish toad is about the same size as the previous species, but is much more flattened and warty. The underside is yellow or orange, splashed with black. This is an example of warning coloration, a visual device advising predators of repulsive-tasting skin secretions. If threatened, the toad arches its back and turns its legs upward to reveal the bright undersides, or even flops over, belly-up.

DISTRIBUTION Much of central and southern Europe.

13

ORIENTAL FIRE-BELLIED TOAD
BOMBINA ORIENTALIS

DESCRIPTION This beautiful species reaches a length of about 2¾ in/69 mm. Its back is an attractive mixture of green and black. However, as with the previous species, it is the underside that is truly startling, the eyecatching mixture of scarlet and black a perfect example of warning coloration. The males sing in chorus at any time of the day or night. The fire-bellied toad (*B. bombina*) of Europe is similar, but darker on the back and slightly smaller.

DISTRIBUTION Southeast Asia.

Aquatic Frogs

Family Pipidae

The 26 species in this family are the most
aquatic of all frogs, spending their whole lives in water.
Their bodies are highly adapted for this, with enormous,
strongly webbed feet allied to robust and powerful legs.
Unlike all other frogs and toads, there is no tongue,
and the eyes and nostrils are set well-up
on top of the head.

SURINAM TOAD
PIPA PIPA

DESCRIPTION When hanging in the water this remarkable toad, with its very flattened body, bears a strong resemblance to a large, decaying brown leaf. Males can reach a length of 6 in/ 150 mm; females are rather larger reaching 6¾ in/170 mm.

During spawning, the male uses his large hind feet to sweep the emerging eggs onto the female's back. Here they become embedded in the soft, spongy skin. After about 15 weeks the thin lid of skin above each egg ruptures, enabling the tiny, but fully developed toadlet to struggle free.

DISTRIBUTION Widespread in tropical South America.

DWARF AFRICAN CLAWED TOAD
XENOPUS TROPICALIS

DESCRIPTION A female of this rather dwarf species can reach a length of 2⅜ in/59 mm or more, but males are smaller. The skin is mostly brownish gray on the back, but lighter on the underside. There is often a broad, irregular brownish-yellow band on top of the head, from the nose to a point well behind the eyes. The head seems rather small for the body, while the hind legs are extremely robust. The common name comes from the three inner toes, which are furnished with small, curved black claws. During the dry season the toads retreat into burrows in the mud. This cocoons them safely until the rains return, when they attach their eggs singly to the submerged stems of waterplants. The tadpoles feed by filtration.

DISTRIBUTION West Africa

Spadefoots, Horned Toads, etcetera

Family Pelobatidae

The members of this rather small and primitive
family are found in North America, Europe, and Asia.
They tend to be quite strongly terrestrial and are usually
found in water only during the breeding season.
The body tends to be rather stout, with
short limbs and large eyes.

COUCH'S SPADEFOOT
SCAPHIOPUS COUCHII

DESCRIPTION The hallmark of the spadefoots is the presence on each foot of a single, sharp-edged black flange of hard skin. This is the spade, used for digging into hard ground. Like the other five members of the genus, Couch's spadefoot is a burrower, escaping from the long droughts of its desert homeland by going underground. When torrential rains return, they trigger a frenzy of mating and egg-laying. This is known as explosive breeding and is found in many other frogs and toads.

Couch's spadefoot is the yellowest species, averaging some 2½ in/63 mm in length. Its spade is elongate, rather than short and wedgeshaped, as in the grayish or brownish plains spadefoot (*S. bombifrons*). The

dark greenish Hurter's spadefoot (*S. holbrookii hurterii*) has a large hump betwen the eyes.

DISTRIBUTION USA, from central Texas to California; Mexico.

ASIAN HORNED TOAD
MEGOPHRYS NASUTA

DESCRIPTION The resemblance to a dead leaf is remarkable, especially the sharp, triangular, leaflike projections above the eyes and nose. This 2¾ in-/70 mm-long species lies in wait, half buried among dead leaves on the forest floor, ready for an unwary meal to walk within range. Prey consists of relatively large and wary animals, such as small rodents, lizards, and other kinds of frogs. There are 21 species in the genus and all except one have tadpoles with very rounded, umbrellalike mouths, used for feeding at the water's surface.

DISTRIBUTION Southeast Asia.

SHOVELFOOT FROGS, TURTLE FROGS, ETCETERA

Family Myobatrachidae

This family contains approximately 100 species
split into some 20 different genera. Their appearance
is amazingly varied and so are their habits: they range
from drab, desert-dwelling burrowers to brilliantly
colored jewels inhabiting wet sphagnum
bogs on mountains.

TURTLE FROG
MYOBATRACHUS GOULDII

DESCRIPTION This strange frog looks like an inflated balloon, its stubby legs and head attached rather incongruously to an oversize body. It is a dirty, dull, brownish gray above and dirty whitish below. When handled it feels like a half-empty and rather saggy bag of water. It reaches a length of 2⅜ in/ 60 mm and uses its short but powerful front legs to burrow in sandy ground in search of termites, its main food. It is often found actually inside termite nests and tends to be found in the open only after rains. The eggs are believed to be deposited in the earth and develop directly into frogs with no intervening aquatic tadpole stage.

DISTRIBUTION The extreme southwest of Western Australia.

GREAT BARRED FROG
MIXOPHYES FASCIOLATUS

DESCRIPTION This chunky frog, with powerful hindlimbs, is usually a rather dark gray or pinkish tan on the upperside, with a series of darker blotches on the head, back, and legs. Although called the great barred frog, its length of 3⅛ in/ 78 mm is about the same as the other members of the genus. The very similar *M. fleayi* often occurs in the same forests, but tends to be a richer shade of brown and has a row of dark spots along the flanks. All species of *Mixophyes* live on the ground in the wet forests of eastern Australia.

DISTRIBUTION Australia, along a relatively narrow coastal strip on the Great Dividing Range from Queensland to New South Wales.

WIDE-MOUTHED TOADS, FALSE-EYED FROGS, ETCETERA

Family Leptodactylidae

This family of over 700 species, in more than 50 genera, is virtually restricted to the Latin American tropics, where it constitutes a significant part of the rich and diverse anuran fauna. One genus, *Eleutherodactylus,* contains over 400 species, making it the largest genus of amphibians and accounting for about 10 percent of all described amphibian species.

NOBLE'S FROG
ELEUTHERODACTYLUS NOBLEI

DESCRIPTION Like most members of this huge genus, Noble's frog is a small (⅞ in/ 21 mm long) and rather nondescript brown frog of the rainforest floor. A broad blackish band down the middle of the back, allied to its general shape, makes it blend in perfectly with the carpet of dead leaves of its home. Members of this genus are primarily terrestrial and generally have no webs between the fingers and unwebbed toes. The fingers are long and thin, with greatly expanded terminal disks. The males call repeatedly from the same spot for long periods. Small numbers of transparent eggs are placed in damp hollows in the ground, among moist, decomposing leaf litter, or in soft, decaying logs. Perfect miniature frogs hatch

from these eggs, and there is no free tadpole stage.

DISTRIBUTION Central America.

CARIBBEAN LEAF FROG
ELEUTHERODACTYLUS MARTINIQUENSIS

DESCRIPTION This small (¹¹⁄₁₆ in/ 18 mm long), putty-colored species has a rather pointed head, with darker lines between the eyes and nose, and a dark line behind each eye. The males are often encountered at night, calling from leaves just above the forest floor, but this frog is also common in the extensive gardens of the larger hotels on many Caribbean islands. Frogs of this genus are mainly sit-and-wait predators, sitting quietly until an insect or spider walks past and then snapping it up in a very rapid movement.

DISTRIBUTION Various Caribbean islands.

ANDEAN FOAM-NEST FROG
PLEURODEMA CINEREA

DESCRIPTION The basic skin color is a muddy brown, blotched, and mottled darker, with a pair of blackish rather eyelike spots on either side of the back towards the rear end. These smallish frogs (length 1¾ in/44 mm) are residents of the High Andes at altitudes of up to 14,530 ft/4,300 m. Here the habitat is arid for much of the year and there are numerous drought-resistant plants, such as cacti. When the summer thunderstorms arrive, thousands of puddles and pools are suddenly created, and these are just as suddenly full of croaking frogs. Egg-laying takes place mainly at night, but is also seen during the day if it is dull and rainy. The legs are used to stir the emerging eggs into a foam, which soon hardens and

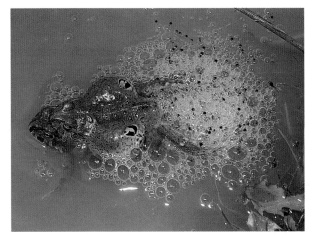

becomes white. Small temporary pools are often half covered in these foam nests after a night's hectic activity.

DISTRIBUTION Andes of South America.

ANDEAN STONE FROG
PLEURODEMA MARMORATA

DESCRIPTION This is rather smaller than the previous species and has a much wartier skin, a very rough and rocklike appearance. It lives in the High Andes among jumbles of rocks and scree, and very much resembles a stone when it hunches down and remains still. Little is known about its breeding behavior, although it certainly does not seem to frequent the same ponds and puddles as the previous species. Although nocturnal, it may be encountered during the day in the rainy season.

DISTRIBUTION Andes of South America.

BELL'S HORNED FROG
CERATOPHRYS ORNATA

DESCRIPTION This is a frog that could aptly be described as all-mouth. In fact the mouth's width is about half the total length of the frog, and the bite is quite powerful and well able to trap any finger that is injudiciously brought too close. The most notable feature of the horned frogs is the long, pointed extension to each upper eyelid, resembling a tiny horn. However, these are not as prominent in Bell's horned frog as in some other species (e.g. *C. cornuta*), making this a horned frog without any horns. The long fingers and toes have no disks and the fingers lack webs. A large male can reach a length of 2¾ in/69 mm, but a hefty female can go up to 4⅝ in/116 mm. Horned frogs half bury themselves in leaf litter and ambush passing prey, such as rodents, frogs, lizards, insects, and spiders. Breeding takes place in ponds and swamps at the start of the rainy season, when the female lays about 500 brown eggs.

DISTRIBUTION Tropical South America.

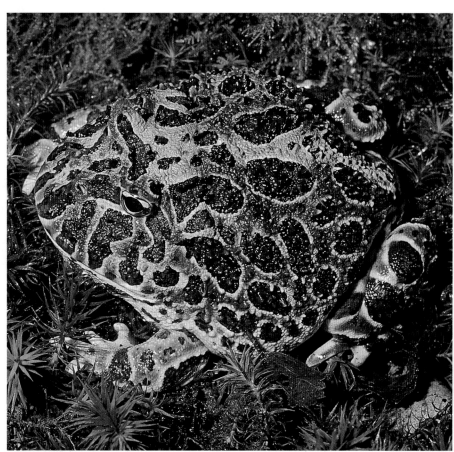

True Toads

Family Bufonidae

The family Bufonidae contains over 300 species
in some 25 genera, distributed worldwide except for
Greenland, Madagascar, and most of Australasia. By far the
largest genus, with over 200 species, is *Bufo*, which also includes
many of the commonest and most familiar toads of the Old
and New Worlds. *Bufo* species have a prominent parotid
gland behind the head, forming an oblong swelling
to the rear of the eyes. This gland secretes defensive
toxins. The females each lay several thousand
eggs, generally in long strings.

FOWLER'S TOAD
BUFO WOODHOUSII FOWLERI

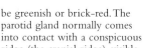

DESCRIPTION This 2–3 in-/ 51–75 mm-long toad can be either gray (as illustrated) or light brown. More rarely it can be greenish or brick-red. The parotid gland normally comes into contact with a conspicuous ridge (the cranial ridge), visible

behind the eye. The underside should be more or less without spots, and there should be three or more prominent warts within each of the largest of the dark spots on the back. The very similar American toad (*B. americanus*), is often found with Fowler's toad, but has dark spots over most of the underside, just one or two warts in each of its dark markings, and no connection (or at most a short spur) between the parotid gland and the cranial ridge.

DISTRIBUTION Over much of the eastern USA (excluding Florida and adjacent areas of Georgia and South Carolina). Replaced to the west by the less distinctively marked Woodhouse's toad (*B. woodhousii woodhousii*).

SONORAN OR WESTERN GREEN TOAD
BUFO DEBILIS INSIDIOR

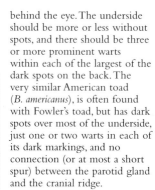

DESCRIPTION Green toads differ from other North American toads not only by their beautiful, bright green coloration, but also by the rather flattened head and body. Although a number of warts are present on the back, they are less prominent than in most other toads, giving the green toads a rather smoother appearance. The warts on the parotid glands and eyelids rise into little black points. In the eastern green toad (*B. debilis debilis*), these warts are broad and flat, and the overall green coloration is also brighter. Both subspecies reach a length of 1¼–2 in/31–50 mm.

DISTRIBUTION A Chihuahuan desert species, from central Mexico northward to Kansas and Arizona. The eastern green toad is mainly found in northwestern Texas and southwestern Oklahoma.

RED-SPOTTED TOAD
BUFO PUNCTATUS

DESCRIPTION The 1½–2½ in-/38–63 mm-long red-spotted toad is unique among North American toads in having round, rather than elongated parotid glands. Cranial crests are generally lacking, although they may sometimes be faintly present. The overall coloration is gray, pale brown, or olive-green, covered with rust-colored warts, and there is no pale stripe down the middle of the back. This is a rather flattened toad, not nearly as rotund as many other species. The males give a loud musical trill during the breeding season. Although often found in deserts, this species is normally found not far from water.

DISTRIBUTION Mainly found in the deserts of the southwestern USA, from southern California to central Texas, and in much of Mexico.

OAK TOAD
BUFO QUERCICUS

DESCRIPTION This dainty little toad only reaches a length of around 1⅜ in/33 mm. Down the middle of the back there is a prominent stripe that can be white, cream, yellow, or orange. Skin color is generally pale gray, with four or five, paired, black or dark brown blotches on the back. In some cases the oak toad may be almost entirely black and unmarked, except for the pale stripe down the back. It is more likely to be seen in daytime than most other toads. The vocal sac of the male is shaped like a stubby and very bloated sausage, and produces a deafening din when used in chorus with other males.

DISTRIBUTION Eastern USA, from Vermont to Louisiana.

SOUTHERN TOAD
BUFO TERRESTRIS

DESCRIPTION The length of this quite large toad usually lies within the 1⅝–3 in/41–75 mm range, but a giant of 4⁷⁄₁₆ in/ 111 mm has been recorded. The head has rather a craggy appearance, bearing two knobbly protrusions behind the eyes in addition to the rather prominent cranial crests. The skin is generally brown, but can be more reddish or almost black, usually sprinkled with darker blotches containing warts. A stripe is usually present down the middle of the back, but this is generally quite faint, and sometimes very indistinct and incomplete. It is mainly found in sandy areas.

DISTRIBUTION Similar to the oak toad (p.27), extending westward to Mississippi.

GULF COAST TOAD
BUFO VALLICEPS

DESCRIPTION This is one of the largest of the North American toads, growing to 2–4 in/50–100 mm in length, with an all-time record of 5⅛ in/128 mm. This is quite an easy toad to distinguish from others occurring within its range, because it is the only one with a dark band along the lower sides. Above this there is a pale brown band, and then the back is generally dark, except for a whitish stripe down the middle.

DISTRIBUTION USA, around the Gulf Coast from Mississippi to Texas, and southward into Central America.

GIANT TOAD
BUFO MARINUS

DESCRIPTION Fully grown adults of this huge, dark brown toad can be distinguished on size alone. The length generally lies within the 4–6 in/100–150 mm range, but giants are quite common, and the biggest of all measured over 9 in/225 mm. The parotid glands form huge elongated bulges, covered in deep pits, and the skin can secrete copious amounts of a powerful toxin. This is unfortunately often fatal to animals, such as dogs, that try to bite the toad. In Australia, where the giant toad was very unwisely introduced to control a beetle pest of sugar cane, it is known as the cane toad and has become a serious pest, poisoning the native snakes that try to eat it. However, some South American snakes eat it with impunity.

DISTRIBUTION Tropical America, northward to southern Texas. Introduced into Florida and several other parts of the world.

NATTERJACK TOAD
BUFO CALAMITA

DESCRIPTION The natterjack is one of only three species of *Bufo* found in Europe (compared with 12 in North America). In exceptional cases it can reach a length of 3¹⁵⁄₁₆ in/ 98 mm, but is more usually 2¾–3⅛ in/69–78 mm. It is generally instantly recognizable by the pale yellow line down the center of the back. This is not found in the common or green toads, but it may some-times be rather faint, or even absent, in the natterjack.

DISTRIBUTION Western and central Europe (including Britain), eastward to Russia.

COMMON TOAD
BUFO BUFO

DESCRIPTION This is the biggest of the three European toads, and females can reach a length of 5⅘ in/147 mm. It is also the most warty and most drably colored, usually in shades of muddy brown, but occasionally reddish, grayish, or olive. There is often a rich pattern of darker blotches, but these can be absent, giving a uniform appearance. In spring common toads are often found during the day, making the long trek to a favorite breeding pond. The eggs are laid in long strings.

DISTRIBUTION Most of Europe (except some of the smaller islands, e.g. Ireland), across Asia to Japan, and in North Africa.

GREEN TOAD
BUFO VIRIDIS

DESCRIPTION This colorful toad somewhat resembles the natterjack (p. 29), but usually lacks any stripe down the center of the back and is generally much more attractively marked with green blotches. Both species are about the same size, but the green toad is rather more robustly built. Unlike the common toad, the males boast an external vocal sac, producing a high-pitched, trilling call that is given in chorus with other males. Like most species of *Bufo,* it is an explosive breeder.

DISTRIBUTION Mainly eastern Europe, northward to southern Sweden, then eastward to central Asia; North Africa.

DEAD-LEAF TOAD
BUFO TYPHONIUS

DESCRIPTION The toads generally grouped under this name seem to belong to a group of several species, known as the *typhonius* complex. Reaching a length of about 2³⁄₁₆ in/55 mm, they all bear a strong resemblance to dead leaves and are seldom seen because they lurk on the forest floor during the day. The crests above the eyes are usually well developed (sometimes much more strongly than in the specimen illustrated), adding to the generally leaflike effect. This is further reinforced by the pointed snout and a sharp-edged spiny fringe around the sides of the body. One form has a bright cream stripe down the middle of the back.

DISTRIBUTION Tropical Americas.

SAVANNAH TOAD
BUFO GERMANI

DESCRIPTION Similar in size to the common toad (p. 30), the savannah toad is a rather variable species. The ground color is usually a rather drab, yellowish brown. Down the middle of the back there is normally a series of dark blotches, although on top of the eyes these form a stripe rather than a blotch. The skin is extremely rough and warty, and the parotid glands are very conspicuous, forming an elongated bulge behind the eyes, which are very bulbous. During the dry season the savannah toad goes into a state of estivation.

DISTRIBUTION Southern Africa.

FUNEREAL TOAD
BUFO FUNEREUS

DESCRIPTION This is another toad that is well camouflaged when in its normal home among dead leaves on the rainforest floor. Its blotchy pattern of white, brown, and black conceals its outline very well against a confused background of dead sticks and leaves. However, it lacks the pointed snout, crests, and spiny fringes of the dead-leaf toad, so is less persuasively leaflike. There is usually a very prominent, pale yellow line down the center of the back. It can grow to about 4 in/ 100 mm in length.

DISTRIBUTION Tropical Africa.

BLACK-SPINED TOAD
BUFO MELANOSTICTUS

DESCRIPTION This is one of the world's most beautiful true toads and can be easily appreciated as it is seldom found far away from human habitations, being especially common in suburban gardens. It reaches a length of about 4 in/100 mm. The female is generally brown and tan, covered with large numbers of small, black-tipped warts. The male's back is usually attractively freckled with rose-pink dots. The eardrum is very conspicuous and usually a beautiful bright pink. The eggs are often laid in garden ponds and drainage ditches.

DISTRIBUTION Southeast Asia.

HARLEQUIN FROG
ATELOPUS VARIUS

DESCRIPTION The 40 or so members of this genus are sometimes included in their own family, the Atelopidae. Considering their appearance, this is not surprising, as they look quite unlike most other members of the Bufonidae, usually having pointed heads, and relatively slim bodies and limbs. The harlequin frog normally bears a bold pattern of black and yellow, and reaches a length of some 1³⁄₁₆ in/30 mm (males) or 1½ in/38 mm (females). However, the coloration is extremely variable and may be green with black markings, or even chiefly black marked with red or yellow (sometimes both together).

DISTRIBUTION Central America.

YELLOW HARLEQUIN FROG
ATELOPUS OXYRHYNCHUS

DESCRIPTION There is little that can be said to expand on the information available in the illustration. This is a bright yellow frog that spends the day sitting around in full view on the rainforest floor. It grows to about 1³⁄₁₆ in/30 mm in length. It shows little or no fear of man, and like all members of the genus, crawls rather than hops when it moves. It is thought that the bright colors of some *Atelopus* species act as warning signals, advertising toxic properties, a system that only works effectively in day-active animals such as these.

DISTRIBUTION Venezuela.

TREE FROGS

Family Hylidae

This is a large family with some 630 species in
37 genera, found all over the warmer parts of the world,
except for Africa, where it is replaced by the Hyperoliidae.
Most species climb well, aided by adhesive, suckerlike
circular disks at the tips of the fingers and toes.
Although many species live in trees or on
low vegetation, others live mainly on
the ground, or even in burrows.

AMERICAN GREEN TREE FROG
HYLA CINEREA

DESCRIPTION A 1¼–2¼ in-/ 31–56 mm-long tree frog that is mainly green but can occasionally be yellow or pale gray, depending on circumstances. There is a fairly broad white stripe around the sides of the body, although this may sometimes fade out towards the rear end, or be absent entirely. The voice is very bell-like and has given rise to local names such as "bell frog" and "cowbell frog."

DISTRIBUTION Eastern USA, mainly along the Gulf Coast plain.

GRAY TREE FROG
HYLA CHRYSOCELIS

DESCRIPTION For our present purposes this description also encompasses *H. versicolor*, also known as the gray tree frog and only separable on voice and small details of internal anatomy. They are rather larger than most North American tree frogs, reaching a length of 2 in/ 50 mm. The color is normally a mottled gray, and the insides of the thighs are yellowish orange, mottled with black. The call is a high-pitched and rather birdlike trill.

DISTRIBUTION Southeastern Canada, through the eastern and central USA to Texas (but excluding Florida).

SQUIRREL TREE FROG
HYLA SQUIRELLA

DESCRIPTION This very variable little frog reaches a length of about 1⅝ in/41 mm. It enjoys a chameleonlike ability to change color, so that the frog you have just found may be green one minute and brown a short while later. It may also be spotted or unspotted. Sometimes there is a dark patch or band between the eyes, and occasionally a pale stripe along the sides of the body.

DISTRIBUTION Eastern USA, from Vermont to Texas, along the Gulf Coast plain.

BARKING TREE FROG
HYLA GRATIOSA

DESCRIPTION This is one of the largest and prettiest tree frogs in North America. It averages around 2½ in/63 mm in length and is quite robustly built compared with the other tree frogs. It is also by far the most heavily marked, with a dense mottling of dark spots against a bright green background. However, under certain circumstances, this mottling can fade away, and the frog is then bright green, or sometimes even pale gray or yellowish brown.

DISTRIBUTION USA, from North Carolina to Louisiana, with a few isolated colonies inland.

PACIFIC TREE FROG
HYLA REGILLA

DESCRIPTION Like so many tree frogs, this is a rather variable species and the situation is further confused by its ability to change color fairly rapidly. The most common color is a plain grass-green with darker markings, although pale brown is also a frequent ground color. The one unvarying characteristic is a dark line running from the nose, through the eye, and back as far as the shoulder. The skin is fairly granular and not as smooth as in some other species. Unlike the mainly arboreal tree frogs, the disks on the finger and toes are not prominent, because this species spends much of its life on the ground. It grows to a length of about 1⁷⁄₁₆ in/37 mm.

DISTRIBUTION Over much of the western USA.

RATTLE-VOICED TREE FROG
HYLA CREPITANS

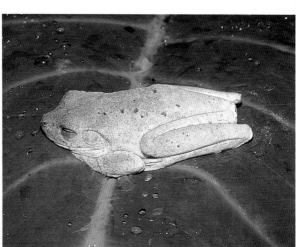

DESCRIPTION This is one of many pale species in which the color varies from night to day. During the day, when the frog hunches down on a leaf in full view, it is almost white. Why such a prominent position is chosen is far from clear. The frog illustrated is sitting in the middle of a large *Philodendron* leaf in Trinidad. It could hardly be more conspicuous, although it does rather resemble a large, splodgy bird-dropping. At night the color changes to a light tan. The males have a very loud, rattling cry, given in chorus.

DISTRIBUTION Northeastern South America; Trinidad.

COMMON TREE FROG
HYLA ARBOREA

DESCRIPTION This 2 in-/ 50 mm-long species is similar to the American green tree frog, except the band along the sides is dark rather than pale. The only other similar European frog is the stripeless tree frog (*H. meridionalis*), which as its name suggests, lacks the lateral stripe. Like most hylids, both species can change color quite rapidly, from the normal light green to dark brown or yellowish.

DISTRIBUTION Most of Europe to Asia Minor.

HARLEQUIN-PATTERNED TREE FROG
HYLA EBRACCATA

DESCRIPTION The harlequin design on this striking little frog (length about 1³⁄₁₆ in/30 mm) is very distinctive and unlike that of any other frog found in the area. The pattern usually consists of brown and yellow, but can also be brown and white, although the hands and feet are always orange. It is an explosive breeder, laying large clutches of eggs on leaves above the water in rainforest swamps. On such a night the frogs are so busy with their frenzy of calling and laying eggs that they often fall prey to the large wandering spiders that are common in their damp habitat.

DISTRIBUTION Central America.

SMITH FROG
HYLA FABER

DESCRIPTION This is quite a large member of the genus, reaching a length of around 3⅛ in/78 mm. The color is normally a pale tan, superimposed with a blotchy pattern of darker brown. There is a white rim around the mouth, and a dark line down the middle of the back. When the frog is at rest during the day (as illustrated), it strongly resembles a fallen dead leaf. The male makes a "nest" by scooping out quite a large crater beside a stream or pool. He attracts females to his prepared

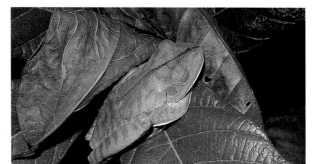

nursery by calling loudly and chasing off any intruding males.

DISTRIBUTION Widespread in tropical areas of South America.

ROUGH-SKINNED TREE FROG
HYLA TUBERCULOSA

DESCRIPTION This is a large *Hyla*, and males reach a length of 3½ in/88 mm, although females are rather smaller. The skin is coarsely granular, more so on the underside than across the back and head. The outer edges of the hands, arms, and feet bear a row of triangular, flaplike outgrowths of skin (just visible on the hind leg in the specimen illustrated). These valances eliminate shadows cast by the frog's limbs, thus helping the body to blend into the small treetrunks on which the frog spends the day.

DISTRIBUTION Over much of tropical South America.

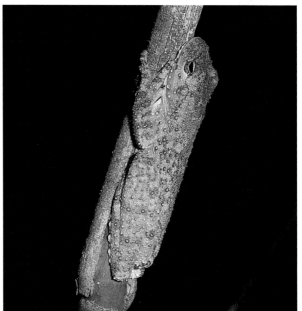

GEOGRAPHICAL TREE FROG
HYLA GEOGRAPHICA

DESCRIPTION The pattern on this frog is simply too variable to describe accurately, because no two individuals ever look alike. However, no other frog within its range looks very similar, so the illustration should be adequate by itself. Note the long "spurs" on the heels, white in the frog illustrated, but just as likely to be brown. This is quite a large *Hyla*, reaching a length of 2⅜ in/61 mm (males) and 3¼ in/81 mm (females). The latter produce nearly 2,500 eggs at a single laying.

DISTRIBUTION Over much of tropical South America.

SARAYACU TREE FROG
HYLA SARAYACUENSIS

DESCRIPTION This pretty little frog was first described from Sarayacu in Ecuador, hence the common name. Males reach a length of 1⅛ in/ 28 mm, females 1⅜ in/35 mm. The basic color is a rich toffee-brown, splashed with variable amounts of yellow. The top of the head is normally one of the few places guaranteed to be yellow, while the yellow on the legs and body may be greatly reduced compared with the frog illustrated. The hands and feet are orange. Breeding takes place in forest ponds.

DISTRIBUTION Widespread in South American rainforests.

ANDEAN TREE FROG
HYLA PULCHELLA

DESCRIPTION The posture exhibited by the frog in the illustration is highly characteristic of this species. Instead of spending the day flattened against a leaf or stone, like most hylids, the Andean tree frog takes up a more upright posture, with its arms folded neatly in front like a miniature Buddha. This 2 in-/50 mm-long frog is basically green, with a brindled pattern of darker markings and a noticeably roughened surface. There is usually a yellow line around the upper lip. The eggs are laid in rivers or temporary ponds generated by the summer rains.

DISTRIBUTION Andes of South America.

TRINIDADIAN GREEN TREE FROG
PHYLLOMEDUSA TRINITATUS

DESCRIPTION This attractive green frog is usually around 2 in/50 mm long, and is one of many similar-looking species in the genus *Phyllomedusa*. However, because this is the only one of the genus found in Trinidad, identification is easy. The eggs are attached to leaves overhanging rainforest pools. As the female deposits the mass of eggs, she gradually uses her legs to fold the leaf over them, forming an elongated pouch.

DISTRIBUTION Trinidad. Many similar-looking species occur throughout the American tropics.

RED-EYED TREE FROG

AGALYCHNIS CALLIDRYAS

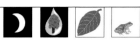

DESCRIPTION With its protruding red eyes and boldly patterned blue and white flanks, this is one of the most beautiful of the tropical American tree frogs. Such "star" quality leads it to being the most frequently featured of all frogs in books, magazines, and on posters. The male is usually only about half the size of the female, which averages about 3⅛ in/78 mm long. The eggs are laid in large masses on leaves overhanging forest pools, but unlike *Phyllomedusa*, no pouch is formed. Upon hatching, the tadpoles simply drop into the water.

DISTRIBUTION Central America.

ORANGE-BELLIED TREE FROG
AGALYCHNIS CALCARIFER

DESCRIPTION When at rest during the day, flattened against a leaf, the speckled green pattern of this rare frog enables it to blend in beautifully with its surroundings, making it extremely difficult to spot. When it moves, it immediately reveals the startling orange undersides, boldly striped with black. This bold uniform is continued onto the inner thighs, which are normally concealed when the frog is at rest. It reaches a length of some 2⅜ in/59 mm. Like all hylids, it crawls rather than hops.

DISTRIBUTION Costa Rica.

SPRING PEEPER
PSEUDACRIS CRUCIFER

DESCRIPTION The spring peeper is a rather nondescript ¾–1¼ in-/19–31 mm-long gray, brown, yellowish, or olive frog. There is usually a dark X-mark on the back, but this is often incomplete or very indistinct, as in the frog illustrated. The other members of the genus are noticeably spotted or striped, so confusion is impossible. The males sing in chorus from beside temporary ponds.

DISTRIBUTION Most of the eastern USA (excluding Florida) and adjacent Canada.

ROCKET FROG
LITORIA NASUTA

DESCRIPTION With its long, pointed face, sleek body, and noted prowess as a jumper, the common name given to this 2 in-/50 mm-long frog should not come as a surprise. Its pattern is very variable, although always in shades of brown, but its general shape should always permit a reliable identification. This is a ground-living species which inhabits the edges of swamps and temporary pools.

DISTRIBUTION Australia, along the wet coastal strip from the Kimberleys to mid-New South Wales; New Guinea.

COMMON BROWN TREE FROG
LITORIA LATOPALMATA

DESCRIPTION This 1⁹⁄₁₆ in/ 39 mm-long frog is another very variable species that is rather difficult to describe. It can be both light or dark brown, with a black band behind the eye and running onto the flanks (as in the specimen illustrated), or perfectly plain. However, behind the thighs, there is always a sprinkling of black spots against a fawn background. This variation may arise because more than one species is currently included under this single name.

DISTRIBUTION Much of eastern Australia, from central Queensland to central New South Wales.

PERON'S TREE FROG
LITORIA PERONII

DESCRIPTION Compared with many members of the genus, this frog has a very granular skin, whose most characteristic feature is a dense stippling of tiny emerald-green spots. When viewed from a distance, these spots tend to merge into the overall, pale brownish coloration, enabling the body to blend beautifully with the lichen-speckled trees on which this frog often spends the day. The inner sides of the thighs and the area of the groin are brightly patterned in black and gold, just visible in the illustration. The body averages about 2 in/50 mm in length.

DISTRIBUTION Over a wide area, both inland and on the coast of southeastern Australia, from southern Queensland to extreme southeastern South Australia.

AUSTRALIAN RED-EYED TREE FROG
LITORIA CHLORIS

DESCRIPTION The eyes of this striking 2½ in-/63 mm-long frog are not always as red as in the specimen illustrated, but can be a fairly pale orange or even gold. The color of the upperside is always a smooth, bright green, while the underside is a beautiful rich shade of golden yellow. The rear edge of the thighs is brown, often with a purplish-red tinge. The disks on the fingers and toes are larger than in many related species. When fully inflated, the golden vocal sac of the male is extremely large and quite spectacular. Males often congregate to sing in chorus from a small bush beside a pond.

DISTRIBUTION Australia, mainly coastal, from central eastern Queensland to mid-coastal New South Wales.

DAINTY GREEN TREE FROG
LITORIA GRACILENTA

DESCRIPTION The illustration shows the characteristic pose adopted during the day by this and most other small green tree frogs. Despite such a cryptic posture, the resting frogs are still found by sharp-eyed predators, such as kingfishers, which pick them off the leaves and swallow them whole in a single gulp. This is one of the smaller Australian tree frogs, averaging about 1¾ in/44 mm in length. The inner sides of the arms and fingers are a bright canary-yellow, while the insides of the thighs are a rich, purplish brown.

DISTRIBUTION Australia, along an extended coastal strip from the tip of Cape York Peninsula to just north of Sydney; New Guinea.

EASTERN DWARF TREE FROG
LITORIA FALLAX

DESCRIPTION This is another small tree frog (length 1 in/ 25 mm), rather similar to the preceding species. The upperside is green all over, sometimes with a sprinkling of darker flecks. There is a dark, bronzy stripe which goes around the side of the snout and then usually, but not always, continues behind the eye for a short distance. A narrow white band circles the upper lip, and the underside of the body is white throughout. The groin region and the backs of the thighs are pale yellow. The northern dwarf tree frog (*L. bicolor*) is very similar, except for a broad bronze band down the middle of the back.

DISTRIBUTION Australia, along the coast and in adjacent inland regions, from central eastern Queensland to southern New South Wales.

GREEN OR WHITE'S TREE FROG
LITORIA CAERULEA

DESCRIPTION This is the largest of the really common green tree frogs, averaging about 4 in/100 mm in length. Despite its specific name (meaning blue), it is not blue, but a bright green, often tinted grayish. There is frequently (as in the specimen illustrated) a rather wobbly white line running from the corner of the mouth to the base of the forearm. The skin is quite smooth and shiny on the back, but rather coarser along the sides. The disks on the finger and toes are large and very prominent. This common frog is often abundant around houses and often lives inside lavatories.

DISTRIBUTION Over most of the northern and eastern half of Australia, not quite reaching Victoria; New Guinea.

GIANT GREEN TREE FROG
LITORIA INFRAFRENATA

DESCRIPTION This is the largest of the Australian tree frogs, averaging about 4⁵⁄₁₆ in/ 108 mm in length. It is similar to the last species, but can be brown as well as green, although the latter shade is much more common. The most distinctive characteristic of this impressive frog is the broad white rim around the lower lip. There is also another white band along the rear margins of the legs, extending onto the fifth toe and partly onto the fourth. As in the green tree frog, the disks on the fingers and toes are very large. The underside is whitish and much more granular than the upperside.

DISTRIBUTION Australia, coastal areas of northeastern Queensland; New Guinea.

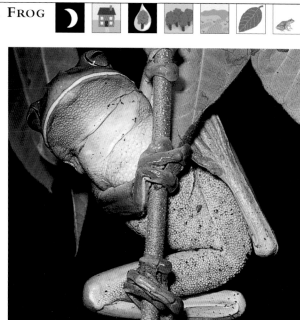

MARSUPIAL FROG
GASTROTHECA RIOBAMBAE

DESCRIPTION This is quite an ordinary-looking frog with extraordinary habits. About 2 in/ 50 mm long, its coloration is basically green, heavily speckled with small black flecks and a mottling of grayish green. It is well camouflaged when at home on the rainforest floor, where spawning takes place. As the eggs emerge from the female, the male uses his back feet to guide them up into a pouch on her back. The capacity of this pouch is remarkable, for it can hold as many as 100 eggs. The tadpoles complete much of their development in this mobile nursery. Eventually the female releases them into some forest pool, scooping out her wriggling brood with her hind feet.

DISTRIBUTION Northern Andes of South America.

WATER-HOLDING FROG
CYCLORANA NOVAEHOLLANDIAE

DESCRIPTION Members of this genus are known for their survival strategy during times of prolonged drought. As the surface waters dwindle away, these frogs cram their bladders full of water and burrow downwards into the rapidly drying mud, away from the heat and drought above. When deep enough, the frog sheds the dead outer layers of its skin, and these form a cocoonlike chamber which reduces water loss to a minimum.

This chunkily built species is basically plain putty colored, with a broad blackish band on either side of the head. It can also be green, with darker flecks (as illustrated). It reaches a length of about 2⅖ in/55 mm.

DISTRIBUTION Australia, from Cape York to northern New South Wales.

SLIPPERY FROGS

Family Pseudidae

The four species of frogs in two genera
that comprise this family are exceedingly difficult to
catch because of the extremely slippery nature of their
skin. They generally resemble the much more
common ranids, and all are strongly aquatic.
Their distribution is restricted
to South America.

PARADOXICAL FROG
PSEUDIS PARADOXUS

DESCRIPTION The common name is derived not from any strange feature of the adult frog, but from the oversized tadpole. This is larger than the frog into which it finally develops. The adult is only some 3 in/75 mm long, yet the bloated black tadpole can reach an astounding 10 in/250 mm in length. The adult is a fairly ordinary-looking frog, with a mostly green head and back, and brown and white limbs.

DISTRIBUTION Trinidad and most of South America.

GLASS FROGS

Family Centrolenidae

This is a relatively small family of 64 species of
generally rather small, semitransparent greenish frogs
which are split into only two genera. The eyes are small
and perched nearly on top of the skull, and there is only
a single tarsal bone in the wrists and ankles instead
of two. Glass frogs are restricted to the tropical
zones of Central and South America.

FLEISCHMANN'S GLASS FROG
CENTROLENELLA FLEISCHMANII

DESCRIPTION With its rather broad, blunt head this is a typical example of a centrolenid. As with many glass frogs, much of the internal anatomy is visible through the translucent skin if viewed from below against a bright light. The tiny males (⁹⁄₁₆ in/14 mm long) sit on the broad leaves of arums and other rainforest plants at night, inflate their vocal sacs and produce a chirping, birdlike call that is remarkable for its volume, given the size of the frogs emitting it. The eggs are laid in masses on leaves overhanging rainforest streams. In some species the male stands guard over the eggs until they hatch.

DISTRIBUTION Central America.

POISON-ARROW FROGS

Family Dendrobatidae

Most of the 120 or so species of frogs in
this family are brightly colored, day-active creatures
of rainforest and cloudforest. Although most species of these
frogs can be quite safely handled, the bright coloration serves as
a warning, advertising the presence of toxins in the skin. In some
species these toxins (known as batrachotoxins) are among the most
deadly of all known poisons. If they enter the bloodstream, they act
on the nervous system, causing rapid paralysis. The dose required
to kill an average-sized human being is several thousand times
less than that required from the most poisonous known snake.
For many years the native peoples of the South American
forests have used these poisons on the tips of their arrows,
hence the common name. The males generally carry
the tadpoles around once they have emerged
from eggs laid on the ground.

ROUGH-SKINNED POISON-ARROW FROG
DENDROBATES GRANULIFERUS

DESCRIPTION This is one of the smallest of the poison-arrow frogs, with males only reaching a length of about ⁹⁄₁₆ in/14 mm; females are rather larger. The skin has a very coarse and granular appearance, making it quite distinct from the smooth-skinned *D. pumilio* (below), which is quite similarly colored. The upperside of the adult is a bright reddish orange, which can be considerably duller than in the specimen illustrated. The underside, hands, and wrists are all a grayish blue, as are the legs, except for a broad, irregular orange band down the tops of the thighs. This pretty little frog can be seen hopping around

among damp, dead leaves on the rainforest floor in daytime.

DISTRIBUTION Costa Rica.

STRAWBERRY OR RED AND BLUE POISON-ARROW FROG
DENDROBATES PUMILIO

DESCRIPTION About the same size as the preceding species, or perhaps slightly larger, this frog is also rather similar in appearance, but has a much smoother skin. Also, the red on the back is continued down onto the undersides, and the limbs are mostly a deep pure blue, rather than bluish gray. There is no orange on the thighs, and there is a variable amount of dark spotting on the back. In one area of Panama an amazing variety of color forms exists, mostly totally unlike the form illustrated (the most widespread form), but too numerous and complex to describe here. The males can often be found engaging in furious combat on the forest floor. The females carry the tadpoles around (usually just one to three, which wriggle up onto the female's back after hatching from eggs laid on the ground). The female climbs up into a tree and places the tadpoles in the small pools of water usually present in many bromeliad plants.

DISTRIBUTION Central America.

GREEN OR TURQUOISE POISON-ARROW FROG

DENDROBATES AURATUS

DESCRIPTION This is a rather larger species, reaching a length of about 1¼ in/31 mm. The specific name (meaning golden) is rather inapt, as the normal colour is a rather strange, metallic green, combined with a shiny, funereal black. Like most poison-arrow frogs, it has little fear of an approaching human. This coloration must be one of the few examples of green being used as a warning color in nature, red, yellow, or blue being more common.

DISTRIBUTION Costa Rica, Panama, and Colombia.

VARIABLE POISON-ARROW FROG

DENDROBATES HISTRIONICUS

DESCRIPTION This is one of the most variable of the poison-arrow frogs, so that different individuals can look like separate species. The body length averages about 1³⁄₁₆ in/ 30 mm, while the coloration is usually black and crimson. However, the crimson color can appear as blotches scattered across a black background, or as stripes. Alternatively, the basic color can be red or orange, with the black merely intruding as a maze of narrow, wavy lines. As with many dendrobatids, there is quite a complex courtship which takes place on the ground.

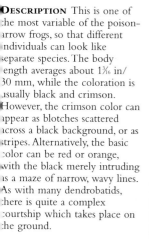

DISTRIBUTION Colombia and Ecuador.

AZURE POISON-ARROW FROG
DENDROBATES AZUREUS

DESCRIPTION This small frog is one of the most spectacularly colored in the world. It is a breathtaking shade of blue, except for a scattering of black and white marks. Like most poison-arrow frogs it has well-developed terminal disks on its fingers and toes, which enable it to scramble around quite easily among the low vegetation of its rainforest home. Most dendrobatids can be recognized by the presence of a pair of platelike projections on the upper surface of the toes and fingertips.

DISTRIBUTION Northwestern South America.

YELLOW-BANDED POISON-ARROW FROG
DENDROBATES LEUCOMELAS

DESCRIPTION The shiny black skin of this 1³⁄₁₆ in-/30 mm-long frog is adorned with a startling yellow pattern. This is rather variable, but often takes the form of a pair of lines across the back, connecting the arms and making it look as though the frog is wearing a belt. The legs are usually also well ornamented with yellow, and so is the head. As with many poison-arrow frogs, this species is often very abundant in the places where it lives, illustrating the effectiveness of the skin toxins in keeping enemies at bay.

DISTRIBUTION Venezuela.

DYEING POISON-ARROW FROG
DENDROBATES TINCTORIUS

DESCRIPTION This spectacular frog reaches a length of about 1¾ in/44 mm. The basic color is black, emblazoned with a brilliant pattern of golden stripes, and the legs and feet are blue with black spots. The common name is derived from the belief (probably a myth) that the native South Americans used the secretions from this frog for dyeing the feathers of pet parrots from green to yellow or red. Such practices do occur in this region, but probably not using this frog as the source of the dye.

DISTRIBUTION Amazonia.

TRICOLORED POISON-ARROW FROG
DENDROBATES TRICOLOR

DESCRIPTION This is another species that looks more like some garish plastic bauble than a living frog. The basic ground color is a bright strawberry-red. From the top of the head, down the middle of the back, to the vent there is normally a yellow stripe. Over the eye and down the sides of the body there is a white stripe, usually fragmented. Another similar stripe runs along the lower part of the body, from nose to thigh. There are a few white splashes on the legs and arms. Like most dendrobatids, this species is

small and probably feeds mainly on ants and other small insects.

DISTRIBUTION Ecuador.

ORANGE-BORDERED POISON-ARROW FROG
PHYLLOBATES VITTATUS

DESCRIPTION An orange line runs from the nose, down either side of the head, across the top of the eye, and back as far as the vent. This contrasts strongly with the very shiny, lacquered finish of the black on the back and sides. The lower part of the sides are grayish blue, speckled with black. The arms and legs are similar, except that the black speckling is much finer and denser. The adults reach a length of about $^{11}/_{16}$ in/18 mm. The males can often be seen with five to six shiny black tadpoles on their backs.

Dendrobates ventrimaculatus from Amazonia is similar, but has an additional orange line down the center of the back and another on either side of the throat. Its limbs are a brighter shade of blue, speckled with quite large black blotches.

DISTRIBUTION Central America.

TRUE FROGS

Family Ranidae

This large family of more than 600 species in
some 40 genera contains many of the species we
commonly know just as "frogs." They are found from
deserts to high mountains, from rainforests to suburban
gardens, throughout the world except Greenland, Antarctica,
New Zealand, and most of Australia. The majority of the
species behave in a conventional way, laying their eggs
in water, where the tadpoles develop. The adults are
generally powerful jumpers and swimmers.

COMMON OR GRASS FROG
RANA TEMPORARIA

DESCRIPTION This is the original frog, being the first of its kind to receive a scientific name, as early as 1758. Like most ranids it has a streamlined shape, with a rather pointed head, goggling eyes, and powerful legs that propel it away from enemies in a leap that would be the envy of many other anurans. The adults can reach a length of 4 in/100 mm, but are generally shorter. Although usually classed as one of the "brown" frogs, the coloration is actually very variable: brown, gray, pinkish, olive, or yellow, usually blotched with black. The scattering of black spots on the back is denser than in any similar "brown" frogs, such as the moor frog (*R. arvalis*), Iberian frog (*R. iberica*), or agile frog

(*R. dalmatina*). All four species are very similar and not easy to tell apart, except by an expert.

DISTRIBUTION Much of Europe (excluding most of Iberia, much of Italy and the southern Balkans), eastward to the Ural Mountains.

AGILE FROG
RANA DALMATINA

DESCRIPTION Although very similar to the common frog, the agile frog is generally rather smaller, seldom reaching a length of 3½ in/88 mm. Its skin sometimes tends to have a translucent quality lacking in other similar frogs, and is generally a fairly unvarying shade of pinkish or yellowish brown. There is usually a scatter of darker blotches, giving the general appearance of a dead leaf. The legs are noticeably dark banded, and the groin is usually a bright yellow. The common frog and moor frog are more robust, with no yellow on the groin and shorter legs. As suggested by its name, the agile frog is a superb jumper.

DISTRIBUTION Widespread in Europe (excluding the British Isles, the Iberian peninsula, and most of Scandinavia).

POOL FROG
RANA LESSONAE

DESCRIPTION Together with several very similar species, the pool frog belongs to the group of so-called "green" frogs. Reaching a length of about 3½ in/88 mm, the coloration is very variable, and can be brown as well as green, usually (but not always) with a pattern of black spots. The backs of the thighs are mottled in pale orange and black, and there is often a pale stripe down the middle of the back. The marsh frog (*R. ridibunda*) is very similar, but very much larger (up to 5⅞ in/ 147 mm long), and the backs of the thighs are mottled with black and pale white. In both species the vocal sacs of the males are mounted on either side of the mouth, rather than beneath the chin. Both species

are also far more aquatic than the common frog, being found in water for much of the year.

DISTRIBUTION Over much of Europe.

EDIBLE FROG
RANA ESCULENTA

DESCRIPTION This is another frog that is very similar to the preceding species, although usually slightly larger (up to 4¹¹⁄₁₆ in/117 mm long). The range of coloration is similar, the male's vocal sacs are whitish and mounted laterally, and the backs of the thighs have similar marbling. The main difference lies in the edible frog's longer legs and a smaller tubercle on the first hind toe. In some parts of Europe males of the edible frog develop yellow heads and backs during the spawning season. The edible frog, pool frog, and marsh frog are all active mainly during the day, and may even sit and bask in the sun.

DISTRIBUTION Much of Europe.

AMERICAN BULLFROG
RANA CATESBEIANA

DESCRIPTION This is a large and impressive creature, usually reaching a length of around 5⅞ in/147 mm, although giants of 7⅞ in/197 mm or more have been recorded. It is usually a rather plain green above, but also often has a rather indistinct pattern of darker markings, these being much heavier in the southeastern USA. Like the African bullfrog, this is a voracious predator with a large appetite. Its capacious mouth is well able to cope with prey such as other large frogs, small mammals, and snakes such as garter snakes. Where it has been introduced into the western states of the USA, this species has exterminated or severely reduced much of the native aquatic fauna.

DISTRIBUTION Native over most of the eastern USA, but introduced in the western states and also in Mexico, Jamaica, Cuba, Italy, and other parts of the world.

SOUTHERN LEOPARD FROG
RANA UTRICULARIA

DESCRIPTION With its boldly patterned body this frog belongs to a group which includes the most handsome of North American ranids. The average length is about 3 in/ 75 mm, about the same as the northern leopard frog (*R. pipiens*). However, the latter lacks a distinct white spot in the middle of the eardrum, has a shorter and less pointed head, and has a greater number of dark spots on the sides of the body. In both species the overall coloration can be green or brown, or a mixture of the two, and the number of dark blotches is extremely variable (sometimes absent). In males of *R. pipiens* the twin vocal sacs are only visible when in use, but in *R. utricularia* they can be seen as loose folds at the sides of the jaws. Both species spend the summer months on land, well away from water, when they can be common in meadows and open woodland.

DISTRIBUTION Over much of the eastern and southern USA.

AFRICAN BULLFROG
PYXICEPHALUS ADSPERSUS

DESCRIPTION The adults are huge (up to 8 in/200 mm long), squat, bizarre, almost turtlelike creatures, with short stubby legs and loose-fitting skin which is heavily corrugated along the back and sides. The upperside is dark green, blotched darker along the ridges of the corrugations. The underside is pale yellow, except under the throat and limbs, where orange tends to prevail. The juveniles (illustrated) look quite different and far less bloated, being attractively blotched in beige and dark green, with a pale stripe down the middle of the back. As can be seen, the corrugations are only weakly developed in the juvenile, which was fortunate to survive to this stage without being eaten by an adult, because cannibalism is rife. Periods of drought are passed in a state of estivation beneath the dried-up lake bottoms.

DISTRIBUTION Over most of sub-Saharan Africa.

MOSS FROG
MANTIDACTYLUS AGLAVEI

DESCRIPTION This remarkable 1¾ in-/44 mm-long frog is a master of the art of camouflage. The top of its body bears a green and brown pattern very reminiscent of moss. The lower edges of the arms and legs are ornamented with soft, wavy-edged frills of skin. During the day, when the frog presses itself against a moss-covered treetrunk, these frills come into play, merging the outline smoothly and imperceptibly into the immediate environment. This renders the frog invisible unless it gives itself away by moving, which it will normally only do if hard-pressed, e.g. if someone accidentally touches it by leaning against the tree. After dark it is not difficult to find a male calling from a leaf above a tumbling forest stream. When a female finally joins him, she lays her eggs on the leaf, and the tadpoles eventually fall into the stream below.

DISTRIBUTION Locally distributed in eastern Madagascar.

Rough-backed Tree Frog
MANTIDACTYLUS ASPER

DESCRIPTION Like the preceding species, this frog is unlikely to be noticed unless it is accidentally disturbed. However, in this case, it is a descending boot that will probably provoke movement, because the rough tree frog lives among the carpet of dead leaves on the rainforest floor, rather than among moss on treetrunks. As the common name suggests, the skin is extremely rough and bears a number of pointed tubercles, of which one pair is particularly prominent, on either side of the back between the legs. The heels bear a flaplike outgrowth of skin (dermal appendage), and the legs are banded with black. Adults reach 1¾16 in/30 mm in length.

Although this species spends most of its time on the ground, the males climb up onto low-growing plants to call during the breeding season. The eggs are laid on leaves and undergo direct development to tadpoles.

DISTRIBUTION Locally scattered in eastern Madagascar.

Golden Mantella
MANTELLA AURANTIACA

enemies. *M. aurantiaca* is probably the best-known species. It is a small frog, only reaching a length of about 1 in/25 mm, with males being smaller than females. Its coloration is a uniform, bright yellow or orange, although the lower surfaces of the legs are bright red. Some specimens may even be a fairly genuine red all over. The males call from the ground in swampy areas of the forest. The eggs are laid in clutches of 20–60 among damp leaf litter, in places where imminent rains will wash the tadpoles into temporary pools.

DESCRIPTION The frogs in this genus are the Madagascan equivalent of the poison-arrow frogs of Latin America. Both types are active during the day and have brightly colored skins that secrete powerful toxins, thereby gaining protection from

DISTRIBUTION Very local in eastern Madagascar; best known at Andasibe.

COMMON MANTELLA

MANTELLA MADAGASCARIENSIS

DESCRIPTION This is by far the most widespread member of the genus and one of the most striking. It is slightly smaller than the preceding species, but has a most memorable and distinguished appearance. The overall color is shiny black, with bright lemon-yellow splashes on the sides of the body, above the point where the arms and legs are connected. The upper surfaces of the legs are decorated with a bold pattern of bright orange, and there is usually a pale yellow stripe along the sides of the head. The males call during the day, usually from some concealed spot among a tuft of grass or from beneath an overhanging boulder, usually near a fast-flowing forest stream.

DISTRIBUTION Quite widespread in eastern Madagascar.

PYGMY FOREST FROG

ARTHROLEPTIS ADOLFIFRIEDERICHI

DESCRIPTION In its size and general shape this tiny frog is rather similar to the *Mantella* species from Madagascar, but is cryptically rather than warningly colored. Life is spent among a carpet of dead leaves on the rainforest floor, where the marbled grayish coloration on the back enables the tiny frog to blend in perfectly until it hops away. Not much is known about the life histories of these frogs, but in at least one species the eggs are placed in a shallow burrow on the forest floor. The diet probably consists mainly of small spiders and tiny insects, such as ants.

DISTRIBUTION Found locally in Tropical Africa.

SEDGE AND REED FROGS

Family Hyperoliidae

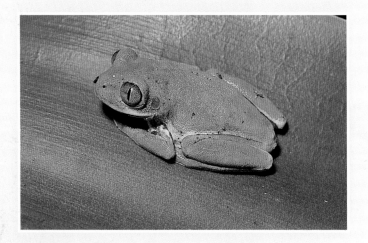

This is a family of some 300 species of
generally small frogs contained in around 23
genera. They are restricted to sub-Saharan Africa,
Madagascar, and the Seychelles, where they basically
occupy the sort of ecological niches normally
taken by the Hylidae.

MARBLED REED FROG
HYPEROLIUS MARMORATUS

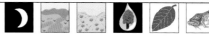

DESCRIPTION A meaningful description of this attractive little frog (¾–1⅟₆ in/19–39 mm long) is difficult as the variation is so great as to be impossible to sum up. The basic color can be green, brown, gray, yellow, or black, and it can be striped, blotched, marbled, spotted, or plain. What is more, these markings can occur in a whole range of colors which vary even within a single population. All in all, this and some of the other 118 species of *Hyperolius* pose a nightmare for anyone attempting to produce a sensible classification. During the day the adults hunch down low on leaves or stems, although they will actively sunbathe on cool mornings.

Most activity happens at night when the males sit beside ponds and call with hugely inflated vocal sacs. The eggs are laid on the submerged leaves and stems of waterplants.

DISTRIBUTION Widespread in southern Africa.

67

ARGUS REED FROG
HYPEROLIUS ARGUS

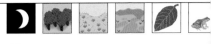

DESCRIPTION This is much less variable than the preceding species, and is normally a pale, semitranslucent gray, marked with large creamy-white blotches. These normally consist of six to seven across the back, three on the thigh (of which one is on the heel), one on each arm and another at the vent. In addition, there is usually a creamy-white V across the nose and up across the eyes. All these pale markings have darker margins, making them stand out very clearly. Adults range in length from ¾–1%₁₆ in/ 20–40 mm. The specimen illustrated is sitting in the daytime posture typical of all reed frogs, many of which can sit like this for hours under a burning sun.

DISTRIBUTION East Africa.

RED-SPOTTED REED FROG
HYPEROLIUS RUBROVERMICULATUS

DESCRIPTION This rare frog shows little variation. The ground color is dark reddish brown, upon which there is a fairly dense sprinkling of red spots and scribbles. On either side of the body, running from the nose to just above the legs, there is a silvery-white stripe, while the heels are also white. Adults range in length from ¾–1%₁₆ in/ 20–40 mm. As depicted here, this species often spends the day on treetrunks, many of which are heavily spattered with reddish lichens, into which the frog blends perfectly. However, this species also spends the day on leaves, where it is more conspicuous.

DISTRIBUTION Kenya, Shimba Hills.

NATAL BUSH FROG
LEPTOPELIS NATALENSIS

DESCRIPTION There are numerous similar-looking members of the genus *Leptopelis* spread throughout tropical Africa. All are basically green, with varying amounts of white on the lips and legs. They spend the day clasped tightly against large leaves near the ground, usually not far from a forest pond or stream. In this respect they are similar to *Hyperolius* (pp. 67–68), as is their generally small size. The eggs are deposited in burrows or hollows beside water.

DISTRIBUTION Southern Africa.

BIRD-DROPPING FROG
AFRIXALUS PYGMAEUS

DESCRIPTION There are 23 species of *Afrixalus*, some of which are as brightly striped as many *Hyperolius*. In the latter the pupil of the eye is horizontal, while in *Afrixalus* it is vertical. *A. pygmaeus* is a small species, only reaching some ¾ in/19 mm in length. It is usually a shiny silvery white, with chocolate-brown on the limbs and along the flanks, and varying amounts of brown blotching on the back. The brown markings are usually peppered with fine white dots. When in its normal daytime resting position on a leaf in full sun (as illustrated), it bears a very strong resemblance to a bird-dropping. The eggs are attached to vegetation above the water.

DISTRIBUTION East Africa.

OLD WORLD TREE FROGS

Family Rhacophoridae

This family contains some 180 species in
10 genera, spread throughout the warmer regions of
the Old World from West Africa to Indonesia and Japan.
These are highly arboreal frogs, often living high
in the tops of towering rainforest trees. The
eggs are usually laid in foam nests.

MALAYSIAN FLYING FROG
RHACOPHORUS REINWARDTII

DESCRIPTION There are several species of flying frogs, although "gliding frogs" would perhaps be a more suitable name. The hands and feet are furnished with a broad fan of webbing that is opened widely as the frog glides from tree to tree. The frog also holds its underside in a concave shape during the glide, which helps to extend the glide's duration. The webbing in this species is black, speckled with blue and green. In the rather similar Wallace's flying frog (*R. wallacei*) the webbing is also black, with contrasting yellow fingers and toes. In both species the body is dark green and the adults grow to about 2⅛ in/55 mm in length.

DISTRIBUTION Malaysia.

YELLOW FOAM-NEST FROG
POLYPEDATES LEUCOMYSTAX

DESCRIPTION The basic color is yellowish brown, with several irregular dark stripes (often broken up into flecks) down the middle of the back, and dark-banded arms and legs. This frog is very common over a huge range and often makes its nests in gardens. The nests, containing about 250 eggs, are normally made on the ground beside a pool that is beginning to fill with water, but they could also be sited on a branch, leaf, or the concrete sides of cisterns and dams. Males reach a length of 2 in/50 mm, but females are much larger, as can be seen from the illustration. This pair were nesting in

daytime in the middle of a path through rainforest.

DISTRIBUTION From the Himalayas to the Philippines.

AFRICAN FOAM-NEST FROG
CHIROMANTIS XERAMPELINA

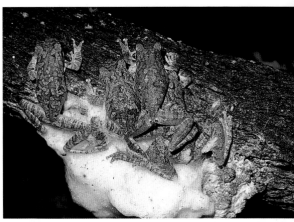

DESCRIPTION During the day this 2–2⅜ in-/50–59 mm-long frog is a light gray, sometimes almost white, usually mottled slightly darker. At night the color darkens to a more brownish gray, with much more pronounced markings. During the dry season the adults sit fully exposed on a branch in the sun, relying for their survival on a skin that is fantastically resistant to drying-out. When the rains come and the waterholes begin to fill, the frogs congregate in some numbers on trees overhanging water. The large foam nests are attached to a branch, and although soft at first, soon form a crust on the outside. This protects the tadpoles within until they emerge from the bottom of the nest as it dissolves. The female normally stands guard on or near the nest.

DISTRIBUTION Central and southern Africa.

BOETTGER'S TREE FROG
HETERIXALUS BOETTGERI

DESCRIPTION This charming little frog reaches a length of some 1 in/25 mm. The general color is bright, glossy green – more yellowish in the males. The hands, feet, undersides of the limbs, and insides of the thighs are all orange, bordered with blue and dotted with black. The adults are easy to find during the day as they sit in full view on leaves beside ponds and swamps, seeming to prefer a site exposed to hot sunshine. This species can be very common where it does occur, but has a very restricted distribution.

DISTRIBUTION Southeastern Madagascar.

LEMON TREE FROG

HETERIXALUS TRICOLOR

DESCRIPTION About the same size as the previous species, the lemon tree frog has similar habits and also spends the day exposed to the heat of the sun on a large leaf. The general coloration is a pale lemon-yellow, usually with a black band through the eye in both sexes, and (in females only) streaks or spots of black across the back. The hands, feet, thighs, and undersides of the limbs are all orange. Nothing is known about the eggs and tadpoles.

DISTRIBUTION Northwestern Madagascar.

DEAD-LEAF TREE FROG

BOOPHIS MADAGASCARIENSIS

DESCRIPTION This is one of the larger Madagascan tree frogs, reaching a length of about 3 in/75 mm (females) and 2⅜ in/ 59 mm (males). The general coloration is the kind of shiny, dark brown characteristic of moist, dead leaves on the forest floor, which this frog strongly resembles. This leaflike appearance is enhanced by the presence of flaplike extensions of skin on the elbows and heels. The eggs are laid in shallow, slow-moving streams in the deep shade of rainforest.

DISTRIBUTION Widespread in eastern Madagascar.

GREEN CASCADE FROG
BOOPHIS LUTEUS

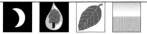

DESCRIPTION The dark green ground color of this 1¾ in-/ 44 mm-long tree frog is covered with a complex network of paler lines. The inner sides of the thighs are often bluish. The iris of the rather goggling eyes has a characteristic red ring around the outer area. The males have paired vocal sacs and usually call from rocks protruding from fast-flowing rainforest streams, or from overhanging leaves beside them. The eggs are attached to rocks or branches in the water.

DISTRIBUTION Eastern Madagascar.

NARROW-MOUTHED FROGS

Family Microhylidae

Found throughout many of the warmer parts
of the world, this family contains about 280 species
in 61 genera. The body is usually stout, with a small head,
narrow, slitlike mouth, and short limbs.
Many species live in burrows;
others are arboreal.

ROT-HOLE TREE FROG
PLATYPELIS GRANDIS

DESCRIPTION The males of this large arboreal frog reach a length of about 3¼ in/81 mm; females are slightly smaller. Adults are generally dark brown, sometimes with a darker, X-shaped mark on the back. The males call from water-filled rot-holes in trees, where the eggs are laid, and subsequently guard the eggs and tadpoles. If the father is removed, the tapoles soon die. As with many frogs, the juveniles are not identical to the adults, and in this case they are mottled and banded with light and dark green. They spend the day flattened against lichen-covered treetrunks (illustrated), where they can be very difficult to spot.

DISTRIBUTION Eastern Madagascar.

TOMATO FROG
DYSCOPHUS ANTONGILI

DESCRIPTION Unlike the brightly colored dendrobatids and *Mantella* species, the tomato frog is a large creature, reaching a length of 4⅛ in/103 mm in females, and plump with it. The red can vary somewhat, from scarlet to rather more orange, but there are no other markings. When handled, the skin produces copious quantities of a milky secretion that can cause an allergic reaction in some people, and presumably renders the frog unpalatable to most predators. Up to 1,500 eggs are laid in still, often stagnant water, sometimes in or near towns.

DISTRIBUTION Northeastern coast of Madagascar.

RAINBOW BURROWING TOAD

SCAPHIOPHRYNE GOTTLEBEI

DESCRIPTION This medium-sized species (females to 1⅜ in/ 34 mm long) is one of the world's most spectacularly colored frogs. There is a broad, rather heart-shaped pinkish-red patch covering much of the back. This is bordered by a blackish area containing islands of greenish yellow. The limbs are white, banded with black, while the underside is also white. No other frog in the world is at all similar. Surprisingly enough, although its rocky habitat is often visited by biologists, the egg and tadpole stages remain unknown.

DISTRIBUTION Isalo Mountains, Madagascar.

MARBLED BURROWING TOAD

SCAPHIOPHRYNE MARMORATA

DESCRIPTION This 1⅝ in-/ 41 mm-long species is spectacular not so much for its coloration but for its amazingly warty and spiny skin. This is particularly noticeable in the males during the breeding season. The general coloration is attractive though subdued: olive to green, with large brownish blotches having indistinct margins. There is no webbing on the hands, and the feet have only a trace. The immature stages are unknown.

DISTRIBUTION Scattered in eastern Madagascar, with one locality in the west.

EASTERN NARROW-MOUTHED TOAD
GASTROPHRYNE CAROLINENSIS

DESCRIPTION Over most of its range there is no other frog with such a peculiar shape and distinctive coloration. The small, rather pointed head is characteristic, along with the rather short limbs and relatively tiny eyes. The general coloration is dirt-brown or gray, usually with a broad, pale reddish-brown band down either side of the back. However, this can be obscured by a mottled darker pattern. The length lies within the range ⅞–1¼ in/22–31 mm. Spawning is initiated by rain, and takes place in ponds and other still waters.

DISTRIBUTION Eastern USA.

PLAINS NARROW-MOUTHED TOAD
GASTROPHRYNE OLIVACEA

DESCRIPTION About the same size as the previous species, this is an easy frog to identify on account of its odd shape and lack of pattern. The skin color varies from gray to tan or olive- green, mainly depending on what the toad is doing and where it is. The only markings are a random scatter of black spots, often present across the back, which look more like some skin infection than a genuine pattern. Skin secretions from narrow-mouthed toads can cause distress in human beings if the fingers are put in the eyes or mouth after the toad has been handled, so it is best to leave them alone.

DISTRIBUTION USA, from Nebraska down through the Great Plains, to southern Mexico.